MW00881508

Crumbs from the Master's Table

Juliet Barnett

Scripture quotations are taken from the KJV Bible

Copyright@2023

Sharon's Creative Enhancements

Cover Design: Brennan Hill

Contents

Foreword

To my dear sister, Juliet, the Lord received my prayer for you. Those who love their children care enough to discipline them. "God loves us." I never doubted that you were God's child; so, I knew there was nothing else I could tell you, so I prayed! The fear of the Lord is to hate evil, pride, arrogance, and the evil way. And the perverse mouth God hates. However, those who seek God diligently will find wisdom. "A wise woman builds her home, but a foolish woman tears hers down with her own hands." (Proverbs 14:1)

The human heart is a place of worship, prayer, and the presence of the Lord. Each heart knows its own bitterness. I have seen you grow closer to God, and I knew He would heal you from past hurts. Remember siblings argue, husbands and wives part ways, and people hold on to past bitterness. God's desire for His children is to forgive one another. God desires a love relationship with you, not perfect behavior. Developing an authentic relationship takes quality time, it does not happen automatically.

God created you to have a personal relationship with Him, His very own daughter. He is patient and will help you grow closer and closer. Juliet, I am so proud of you and thank God for giving you His wisdom and revealing His truths so that you may share with the world. Fear of the Lord is a life-giving fountain; it offers escape from the snares of death. As believers, we are to confess our wrongdoings to God, no matter how others treat us-then receive his forgiveness. God is in control of Heaven and Earth. Because God's word is true, when we chose to love others, treat them with respect, and forgiveness, God will strengthen you to display His love.

Love forever, your sister in the natural and in Christ.

Mrs. Lola Lunford

Acknowledgments

This book is precious to me, because it is my first in the series of "Crumbs from the Master's Table." Secondly, it reflects my own story. I am thankful for all the people who have supported me in my Christian journey, thus far, bringing me to this day.

Special thanks to Pastor Lorraine Bingham, my first Pastor and the one who led me to Christ. She taught me the fundamentals of prayer.

Sincere and precious thanks go to my current pastors, Ambassadors Ricky, and Pastor Sheila Floyd for all their encouragement and support. They are the continually leading me to pray and teaching me the truths of the Bible.

I give heartfelt gratitude to my family: Phinikki, Jacorian, Jacorianna, Alyssa, and Alayia, Charley, Travis, Chyna, and Callie for all their love, patience, and support. You are loved and appreciated more than you know.

Finally, I give thanks to my publisher Pastor Sharon Fields of Sharon's Creative Enhancements for making this happen for me.

Special Dedication to Jesus

Dear Jesus,

Thank you for saving me and giving me a place at your table" forever," and for reminding me constantly, that I am your dear child. Help me to always praise and trust you. Fill me Holy Spirit with love, gentleness, and kindness towards others. Teach me to submit to the leading of the Holy Spirit as I am being transformed.

Join me in praising God for His glorious acts. Father God, I praise you for your love, forgiveness, salvation, kindness, mercy, wisdom, direction, advice, healing, and your tenderness. We receive all these freely, without having to earn any of them. No matter how difficult one's life seems, there is always a reason to be grateful. Remember, "Enter His gates with thanksgiving and into His courts with praise. Give thanks to Him and praise His name" (Psalms 100:4). Heavenly Father, I thank you for the wisdom, courage, knowledge, and patience to author this book. All the glory belongs to you.

Love,

Juliet Barnett

Opening: "The Way She Was"

There is nothing sweeter and more delightful in this world than a continual conversation with God. When we experience trouble, the first thing we do is complain. Complaining simply means we are unhappy with the present situation and think telling others that we want it to change. There is a difference between having an honest discussion about a situation instead of complaining about it.

As we read the book of Psalms, we can see David and the other psalmists share their concerns with God. They hold nothing back and it appears as though they are complaining but they are praying. (Crumb)

The motivation behind our complaining is the key issue. Many times, we complain about issues to gain attention from others. Sometimes we complain or ask God for help because of a wrong choice that has yielded a negative consequence. The natural response is to ask God to get us out of it. Although, God always hears us, he knows that the solution is not always coming to our rescue. Some troubles are best solved by being humble and being accountable for our part in the situation. And if trouble comes from people or situations that are beyond our control, God is not only quick to hear but also quick to respond.

We all have a past and no, we cannot change what happened, but we can change our perspective. With the power of prayer, we can learn from our past, find healing, and be thankful for the good times God gives. Jesus can redeem our past, no matter what type of past we bring to the table.

Whether we are the one who messed up-or someone wounded us, we can give our past to the Lord. It is a mystery how that transformation happens, but when we pray about our yesterdays, we can find healing for today and hope for our future. Do you remember when you used to daydream as a child, what you wanted to be when you grew up? Whatever the reason, it is never too late to dream again and discover God's will for the next season of our lives. Praying for our goals begins with surrendering them to God, being willing to except His plan no matter the outcome.

As we seek God's will for our dreams and goals, we ask Him to confirm if we are headed in the right direction. "If the Lord delights in a man's way, he makes his steps firm" (Psalm 37:23). Prayer is the key to reaching our goals no matter what phase of the journey we are in planning, working, or living the dream.

When we commit our dreams to God (Psalm 37:4-5), we can pray powerfully with sincere and surrendered hearts. John 1:17 says, "God's unfailing love and faithfulness came through Jesus Christ." It is my hope that "Crumbs from the Master's Table" reminds you that He is always faithful and always there. The eternal love of Jesus is a source of nourishment for our spirit. He wants to refresh you each day and know that He is concerned about the big and trivial things in your life. "Crumbs from the Master's Table" will help you rediscover His comfort and care through reflections of hope, faith, and love.

NEW EXPERIENCES
NEW ADVENTURES

Scripture Focus: "I, yes, I alone am he who blots away your sins for my own sake and will never think of them again." (Isaiah 43:25)

One of my favorite verses to meditate on is Isaiah 43:19 for I am about to do something new. See, I have already begun! Do you not see it? These words feel me with excitement the same way hanging a new calendar on the wall does. A New Year stretch is ahead with new experiences and adventures, new friends to make, fresh opportunities to serve Christ and grow to be more like him.

But cleaning out my pantry last week helped me to understand that before we can embrace the new, we may need to get rid of some of the old. Before we make plans for the New Year ahead, we would do well to engage in some serious self-evaluation to see what we need to get rid of habits that compromise our walk with Jesus Christ. Doubt keeps us from using our gifts to fully serve him. And especially guilt, shame, condemnation, and regret, overpass failures and sins. Just a few verses after God promises to do new things, we see his promises not only to forgive when we repent but to never think about them again.

Crumb#1: Ask Jesus to show you what you need to throw out so you can fully receive the new things he has planned for you.

A BEAUTIFUL WORD
PICTURE OF HOPE

Scripture focus: "I cried out to the Lord, and he answered me from his holy Mountain."(Psalms 3:4)

As an English instructor and writer, I am very fond of the American poet Emily Dickinson. She made it a beautiful word picture of Hope when she wrote, "How is the thing with feathers- that purchase in the soul- and sings the tunes without the words- and never stops at all." Some correctly captured the essence of sincere hope when she said it never stops at all. Hope is that ongoing realization that tells our hearts that things can get better; that someone other than us, has things under control, and that whatever had that thing we were enduring, something better lies ahead. Here is an example of how new hope can lift the heart of one who is facing insurmountable hopelessness.

In Psalms 3, King David has just discovered that his son Absalom has a man in an army to take over the throne. How many are my falls! David says as he will realize the seriousness of the threat and he has heard that the people of Israel have concluded God will not deliver him first. Yet David praised God, whom the king calls a shield around me. He also realizes that when he calls out for help, God answers him from his holy Mountain. And he concludes that the Lord is so strong and mighty, and from the Lord come deliverance. David understood that with God hope never stops at all.

Crumb #2: We can always have confidence that our heavenly Father, cares deeply for us, because Hope never stops at all.

WHEN MORNING COMES

Scripture focus: "Now faith is confidence in what we hope for, insurance about what we do not see." (Hebrews 11:1)

Sometimes life can get clouded as a heavy fog of despair. Our situation may look so dark that we began to lose hope, but just as the sun burns away fog, our faith in God can run away to rays of doubt. Hebrews 11 defines faith as confidence in what we hope for, an assurance about what we do not see. The passage goes on to remind us of the faith of Noah, who was worrying about things not seen yet obeys God. "By faith Noah, being warned of God of things not seen as yet, moved with fear, prepared an ark to the saving of his house; by the which he condemned the world, and became heir of the righteousness which is by faith."(Hebrews 11:7-8) that we have not seen God I cannot always feel his presence, he is always present and will help us through our darkest nights.

There was a time a couple of years ago when I was down on myself and very confused. I could not do anything to make myself feel better. So, I prayed about it! One night I opened my Bible looking for help. I scanned through the book of Psalms remembering a Christian friend. As he once told me that whenever he felt bad; reading Psalms would help him. Something jumped off the page at me as well, especially verse three. I am sick at heart how long O' Lord until you restore me? That is how I felt, totally distressed. I read and reread that psalms many times. It spoke straight to my heart, and it showed me that God was there for me always. Now, when I am in doubt about God's love and care for me, I turn to that psalms. It reminds me that God is always there and that he will lead me through every dark encounter that I may experience, just as he did on that night.

Extra Crumb on the table: Made in the image of God: got a coin handy? Good. Whose face is on it? More than likely, you are looking at an image of a former president or well-known woman from history; Susan B. Anthony of Saskatchewan. If you check out a set of stamps long enough you might see the image of another well-known person from history. Imagine having coins or stamps bearing your image. Unfortunately, you must be dead before you can appear on either.

Although God has never been on a stamp or coin, many people bear his image. According to Psalms 8, we were made in his image and likeness. We are stamped with his likeness. This does not mean that we have his chin or eyebrows, but we have his characteristics. It is easy to believe this truth when we think about kind, attractive, and thoughtful people. But it is just as true of the murderer on death row, or the terrorist who bombs airports. We are God's image bearers not because we are good but because he created us.

Sometimes we are confronted by people who seem to exist only to make our lives unpleasant; the classmate who majors in being obnoxious, the relative who constantly criticizes you, the teacher who takes pleasure in correcting you, and the bully. We must remember that person was made in God's image just as you are. Regardless of our habit of wrongdoing, we have an immense value to God.

IT IS IN THE BLUEPRINT YOU MUST SUFFER

Scripture focus: "And how is it written of the son of man, that he must suffer many things, and be sat at naught." Mark 9:12.

My beloved because you are close to me you must share my life. Not only will you know my joy in my peace, my love and my courage, my zeal, and my vision, you will also know my suffering.

There is much suffering for those who live close to me. Every pain that I feel, they also feel. Every nail that pierces me, pierces them. If you seek to escape suffering, you will find yourself far from me. If you walk with me, you will find yourself in the garden of the trail, in the walk halls of condemnation. Others less great than yourself shall condemn you and pass judgment on you. They do this because they do not know me. If they knew me, they would surely know you, like I know you and they would love you like I love you.

It was written of my forerunner that he must suffer, and he accomplished it and fulfilled his blueprint. It is decreed of you, as my close followers, to also drink my cup and know my bitterness and rejection. To this day, you have fulfilled this pattern, but when it is over, you will rejoice because you were counted worthy to know me in the fellowship of My suffering. You shall also know Me in the power of My resurrection.

Crumb #4: The truth you teach is love.

LOVE THOSE DISCIPLINES

Scripture focus: "We also glory in our sufferings because we know that suffering produces perseverance; perseverance character; and character hope." (Romans 5:3–4).

My friend, Jesse was riding his motorcycle when a car swerved into his lane and pushed him into an oncoming traffic. When he woke up two weeks later in the trauma center he was a mess. Worst of all, he suffered a spinal cord injury that left him a paraplegic. Jesse prayed for healing, but it never came. Instead, he believes that God has compassionately taught him that the purpose of his life is that he become conformed to the image of Christ. This happens when life is tough. We are forced to rely on God through prayer just to make it through the day. This was terrible; I did not know what to do.

The Apostle Paul explained two benefits of right standing with God: persevering and rejoicing in suffering according to Romans five. These benefits were all a call to endure suffering with strong fortitude or to find pleasure in pain. It was an invitation to unshakeable confidence in God. Suffering plus cries, cultivates perseverance, character, and hope. This all flows from a faith that the Father will not abandon us, but will walk with us through the fire and into the future. God meets us in our sufferings and helps us grow in them. Rather than viewing afflictions as his disfavor, look for ways he is using them to sharpen and build our character, as we experience his love poured out in our hearts.

Crumb #5: Jesus, may I find hope and joy in you as you provide what I need to persevere in this life.

SUCCESS AND SACRIFICE

Scripture focus: "This is how we know what love is: Jesus Christ laid down his life for us."(I John 3:16)

During my college years, I read a book about a boy who wanted to climb the Alpine Mountains in Switzerland. Practicing for this goal occupied most of his time and when he finally set out for the summit, things did not go the way he planned. Partially up the slope, a teammate became sick, and the boy decided to stay behind to help him, instead of achieving his goal.

Upon returning to the classroom, our teacher asked, "Was the main character a failure because he did not climb the mountain?" I was so surprised at the responses one student gave, He said, "yes, because it was in his DNA to fail." Another student quickly disagreed; and reasoned that the boy was not a failure because he gave up something important to help someone else. I totally agree with this person. When we set aside our plans and care for others instead, we are acting like Jesus. Jesus sacrificed having a reliable income and social acceptance to travel and share God's truth. He gave up everything and ultimately he gave up his life to free us. He showed us God's love.

Earthly success is much different from success in God's kingdom. He values the compassion that moves us to rescue disadvantaged and hurting people. He approves of decisions that protect people and with God's help we can align our values with his and devote ourselves to loving him and others, which is the most significant achievement, one can achieve.

Crumb #6: Holy Father, I want to be successful in your eyes teach me how to love others the way you love me.

CRUMB ON THE TABLE!

We were created to worship. Sing our songs of praise to God, as our Creator, Savior, Provider Healer, Redeemer and Deliverer. Reading Psalms can encourage us to praise God. God is all powerful, and always in control of every situation. Believing in God's power we can overcome the despair of any painful trial. Many of the Psalms are intense prayers, asking God for forgiveness. Because God forgives us, we can pray to him honestly and directly, When we receive God's forgiveness, we move from being separated from him to being close to him, from feeling guilty and shameful, to feeling loved.

God protects, guides, forgives, and provides everything we need. When we realize how much we benefit from knowing God, we can fully express our thanks to him. God's faithfulness and justice have been proven throughout history. Knowing him intimately, drives away doubts, fear and loneliness. The book of Psalms presents a clear picture of God. Our emotions change constantly but God is constant. While we fret, worry, and shout about injustice, God remains calm. When we come to him embarrassed because of something we did wrong, he does not express surprise or anger. Psalms reminds us that God is exalted, the Creator and ruler of the world, and worthy of worship.

REMEMBERED IN PRAYER

Scripture focus: "Then God remembered Rachel; he listens to her."(Genesis 30:22)

In the large African church, the pastor failed to his knees praying to God. "Remember us", the pastor pleaded and the crowd responded crying, "remember us Lord!" Watching this moment on YouTube, I was surprised that I cried too. The prayer was recorded earlier, yet it recalled childhood times when I heard our family's pastor make the same plea to God, "remember us Lord". Hearing their prayers, as a child, I could only assume that God sometimes forgets about us, but God is all knowing. He always sees us, and he loves us beyond measure. Even more, as we see in the Hebrew word Zakhar, meaning "remember", when God remembers us he acts for us. Zakar also means "to act on a person's behalf". Thus, when God remember Noah and all the wild animals and livestock that were with him in the ark, he then sent a wind over the earth and the waters receded according to Genesis 8:1. When God remembered a barren Rachel, he listened to her and enabled her to conceive. She became pregnant and gave birth to a son (Genesis 3:22-23). I sat there as I remembered how God remembered me as I cried and cried and as he helped me to trust him to let go of my other security blankets. What a great plea of trust to ask God in prayer to remember us! He will decide how he answers. We can pray knowing that is an humble request asking God to move!

Crumb #7: This do in remembrance of me. Then, when and where I need you to act, please remember me again.

WASHED

Scripture focus: "You were washed, you were sanctified, and you were justified in the name of the Lord Jesus Christ." (I Corinthians 6:11)

My best friend Choley describes Gertrude, an acquaintance of hers, as being extremely far from God. One day after Choley left, I decided to try something different with Gertrude. I begin to explain to her how God's love has provided the way for us to be saved. She became a believer in Jesus Christ. Through tears she repented of her sins and gave her life to Jesus Christ. Afterwards Choley asked Gertrude how she felt, wiping away tears, she answered "simply washed".

I thought to myself, "what an amazing response". That is exactly the essence of salvation. Only possible through faith in Jesus' sacrifice for us on the cross. In I Corinthians 6, after Paul gives examples of how disobedience against God leads to separation from him he says "this is what some of you were, but you were washed, you were sanctified, you were justified in the name of the Lord Jesus Christ". Washed, sanctified, and justified; words that point to believers being forgiven and made right with God.

Titus 3:4–5 tell us more about this miraculous thing called salvation. God, our Savior, saved us not because of righteousness, but because of his mercy. He saved us through the washing of the rebirth. Sin keeps us from God and through our faith in Jesus; the sin penalty is washed away. We become new creations, gain access to our Heavenly Father, and are made clean. He alone provides what we need to be washed.

Crumb #8: Dear Jesus, I know I have sinned against you, and I realize that the penalty for sin is separation from God. Thank you for the salvation you made possible and for drawing me close to you, forever, and ever.

ETCH-A-SKETCH FORGIVENESS

Scripture focus: "As far as the east is from the west, so far has he removed our transgressions from us."(Psalms 103:12)

I was so happy on Christmas morning to be the first person awake. I hurriedly went into Chyna's room to wake her up. She glared at all the wonderful gifts she had and then she grabbed a little red rectangular box. She opened it; it was an

Etch-a-Sketch. It seems to be magical; when she turns one knob she could create a horizontal line on its screen. When she turned the other knob a vertical line, but when she turns the knobs together, she can make diagonal lines, circles, and creative things and designs. The real magic came when she turns the toy upside down, shook it, and turn it right side up. A blank screen appeared, offering her the opportunity to create an innovative design.

I thought to myself, "God's forgiveness work so much like that". He wipes away our sins, creating a clean canvas for us. Even if we remember wrongs we have committed God chooses to forgive and forget. He has wiped them away and does not hold our sins against us. He does not treat us according to our sinful actions but extends grace to forgiveness. We have a clean slate a new life awaiting us, when we see God's forgiveness. We can be rid of guilt and shame, because of his amazing gift to us. In God's eyes, sin no longer clings to us like a scarlet letter or a bad drawing. This is reason to rejoice and to thank God for his amazing grace and mercy.

Crumb #9: Loving God, thank you for your forgiveness and for reminding us daily that you no longer remember our sins.

A CRUMB ON THE TABLE

"Not by power, not by might, but by my spirit", says the Lord. Because of the dark days ahead, God sees that we need a special word to strengthen us and encourage us to press on. In the past year, the Lord has been speaking to me many mornings and sometimes in the evenings. I felt I should share this revealed hidden truth. If you feel parts do not apply to your life put it on the side on the shelf let God speak to you where he can. His one desire is to daily give us the preparation we need so that we may be perfect, and be counted worthy to be his bride.

Scripture reading: Zachariah 4:1–14. "Then he answered in speaking to me, saying this is the word of the Lord onto Zerubbabel saying not by might nor by power but by my spirit says the lord of host (Zachariah 9:6) who art thou oh majestic mountain? Before Zerubbabel shall become a plain: and he shall bring forth the hate stone thereof with shouting, and crying, grace onto it. Moreover, the word of the Lord came out to me saying the hands of Zerubbabel have laid the foundation of his house; his hands you will also finish it; and then she will know that the Lord of Host have sent me onto you. It is the anointing, that golden oil of the Holy Spirit, which is your help, for every one of your needs."

Man may seem to be immensely powerful, like the enemies of the Riverdale. They may use every method conceivable to manage God's plan but do not lift one hand to fight back with this flesh and blood enemies. Cry to the Lord for a mighty deliverance through the power of the Holy Spirit. My Holy Spirit will work mightily to remove every mountain of hindrance. Your own mighty power is nothing compared to my mighty power. Put me on your case and watch me work for you. Have you like Zerubbabel begun to build a great building for me? My child, you shall through the power of my Holy Spirit also complete this building. My spirit is striving, speaking, dealing, and working with many disobedient, faithless greedy hearts to bring in the finances for the complete structure of this building. I will not give them peace until they obey, and if they never obey; then they will never have my peace, for it is my building they are building. But by my spirit, I will complete all that I have begun to do.

Many, who think they are honest, steal from God taking the tithe which belongs to the Lord and keeping it for them. It does not belong to them, yet they steal it from the Lord as Malachi, my prophet stated in Malachi 3:-9. They swear falsely by my name and this great judgment of the end-time shall be upon those who steal and those who swear falsely by my name.

STAY AWAKE

Scripture focus: "Watch and pray so that you will not fall into temptation. The spirit is willing, but the flesh is weak." (Matthew 26:41)

Look at this Face book post! A German bank employee was in the middle of transferring €62.40 from a customer's bank account when he accidentally took a power nap at his desk. He goes off while his finger was on the "2"-key, resulting in 822 €2 million, $300 million transferred into the Customer's account.

Jesus warned his disciples if they did not remain alert, they would make a costly mistake. He took them to a place called GETHSEMANE to spend some time in prayer. As he prayed, Jesus experienced a grief and sadness such as he had never known in his personal life. We read in Matthew 26:38 where Jesus asked Peter, James, and John to stay awake and pray and keep watch with him but they fell asleep. Their failure to watch and pray left them defenseless when the real temptation of denying him presented itself. In the hour of Jesus' greatest need the disciples lacked the spiritual vigilance. Maybe we need to heed Jesus' words to remain spiritually awake by staying more devoted to spending time with him in prayer. As we do, he'll strengthen us to resist all kinds of temptations and avoid the costly mistake of denying Jesus.

Crumb #10 Jesus, because I have been spiritually sleeping, I have not been praying fervently, and I have not been totally depending on you. I'm apologizing now help me to spend more time with you every day.

GIVE WHILE YOU LIVE

Scripture focus: "As long as it is day we must do the works of him who sent me." (John 9:4)

Look, what was in the news! A successful businessman spent the last few decades of his life doing all he could to give away his fortune. A multi billionaire, donated cash to a variety of causes such as bringing peace to northern Ireland and modernizing Vietnam's healthcare system: not long before he died he spent $350 million to turn New York City's Roosevelt Island into a technology center. The man said, "I believe strongly in giving while living." I see a little reason to delay giving, besides it is a lot more fun to give while you live than to give when you are dead. Give why you live, what an amazing attitude to have.

In John's account of the man born blind, Jesus' disciples were trying to determine who sinned. Jesus briefly addressed their questions by saying, "neither this man nor his parents have sinned but this happened so that the works of God might be displayed in him. As long as it is day, we must do the works of him who sent me." Though our work is very different from Jesus' miracles, no matter how we give of ourselves, we are to do so with a ready and loving spirit. Whether through our time, resources, or actions, our goal is that the works of God might be displayed. For God so loved the world that he gave. In turn, let's give while we live.

Crumb#11: Giving God, please show me people or places where I can give today.

WE ARE ONE

Scripture focus: "Do not conform to the pattern and dictates of this world, but be transformed by the renewing of your mind."(Romans 12: 2)

I was born in a small farming country in a town called Rosedale Mississippi. In a small farming community, news travels fast.

Several years after the bank sold the farm my brother, Nathan, learned the property will be available for sale. After much sacrifice and saving, Nathan arrived at the auction and joined a crowd of nearly 200 local farmers. Was Nathan's meager bid, big enough? He placed his first bid, taking deep breaths, as the auctioneer called for higher bids. The crowd remained silent until they heard the slam of the gavel. The fellow farmers placed the needs of Nathan and our family above their own financial advancement.

This real life story reminds us about the farmers', sacrificial act of kindness and demonstrates the way the Apostle Paul urges followers of Christ to live in this world. Paul warns us not to conform to the patterns of this world, by placing our selfish desires before the needs of others, and scrambling for self preservation. Instead, we can trust God to meet our needs as we serve others. As the Holy Spirit, renews our minds, we can respond to situations with God honoring love and motives. Placing others first can help us to avoid thinking, too highly of ourselves as God reminds us that we are part of something bigger - the church. The Holy Spirit helps believers understand and obey the scriptures. He empowers us to be unselfish in our giving and to love generously so that we can thrive.

CRUMB ON THE TABLE! Keeping it real:

Nothing hurts as much as a wound from a friend. Real friends however, stick by you in times of trouble and offer love, acceptance, and understanding. There will be times when friends lovingly confront us, but their motive will be to help.

As king of Israel, David had met many, who pretended friendship for selfish reasons. David knew God would punish accordingly, but he prayed that their punishment would come swiftly. It's easy to pretend friendship. Deceitful people often pretend to be kind or offer a false sort of friendship to gain their own needs or ends. True believers live honest lives before God and others. They do not offer friendship with wrong motives.

Have you ever been falsely accused by someone and wanted revenge? David wrote a Psalm to address this when he was falsely accused of trying to kill King Saul to gain the throne. Read

1Samuel 24:9-15. Instead of seeking revenge David cried out to God for justice. The proper response for false accusations is prayer not revenge.

God says; "I will take revenge, I will pay them back". (Deuteronomy 32:35) Instead of striking back ask God to right your wrong and restore your reputation. This study was definitely a "Crumb from the Master's Table" for me. Now I pray for that person whom I thought was a friend. I have now learned to pray that God rights my wrongs and restores my reputations.

LISTEN AND LEARN

Scripture focus: "Everyone should be quick to listen, slow to speak, and slow to become angry."(James1:19)

Going on a particular street in Cordova, I noticed one side of the street, a homeowner displays in his yard a giant blowup bald eagle draped in a US flag. A big truck sits in the driveway, its side windows featured a painted flag, and the bumper is covered with patriotic stickers. Directly across the street in another neighbor's yard are signs that highlight slogans for current social justice issues that have been publicized on the news and social media. Are the people of these homes feuding or friends? We might wonder, is it possible that both families are believers in justice. Call causes us to live out the words of James 1:19. Everyone should be quick to listen, slow to speak, slowly to become angry. Too often, selfish ways definitely hold on to our opinions and are willing to consider what others are thinking. Matthew Henry's commentary has this to say "We should be swift to hear a reason in truth of all size and be slow to speak and when we do speak, it should be nothing of wrath." Someone has said learning requires listening. The practical word from God in the book of James can only be accomplished if we're filled with God's loving spirit, and choose to respect others. He is willing to help us make changes in our hearts and answers. Are we open to listen and learn?

Crumb #13: You know me, God. I can be very opinionated at times. Father God, help me to be quick to listen, slow to speak, and slow to anger.

PREJUDICE AND FORGIVENESS

Scripture focus: I now realize how true it is, that God does not show favoritism. (Acts: 10:34.)

Today, Pastor Todd delivered a powerful message on prejudice and forgiveness. Everyone seemed to really enjoy the message.

After hearing this message about correcting injustice, one of our church members approached, the pastor, weeping and asking for forgiveness and confessing that he hadn't voted in favor of calling the black minister to be pastor of the church because of his own prejudice. "I really need you to forgive me", he said. "I don't want the junk of prejudice and racism spilling over to my kids lives." I didn't vote for you and I was wrong. His tears and confession were met with the tears and forgiveness of the minister.

A week later, the entire church rejoiced upon hearing the man's testimony of how God had changed his heart and cleansed him of prejudice.

Even Peter, a disciple of Jesus, and the chief leader in the early church, had to be corrected because of his ill-conceived notions about non-Jewish people. Eating and drinking with Gentiles, who are considered unclean, was a violation of social and religious protocols.

Peter said, "You are well aware that this is against our law for a Jew to associate or visit a Gentile." (Acts 10: 28) It took nothing less than a supernatural activity of God to convince him that he should not call anyone impure or unclean. Through the preaching of scripture, the conviction of a Holy Spirit, and life experiences, God continues to work in human hearts to correct our misguided perspectives about others. He helps usto see that God does not show favoritism.

Crumb #14: "I need to change, God has no favorites"

GOOD TROUBLE

Scripture focus: "But let justice roll down like waters, and righteousness like an ever- flowing stream" (Amos 5:24)

When John Lewis, an American congressman and civil rights leader, died in 2020, people from different political persuasions mourned. In 1965, Louis marched with Dr. Martin Luther King Jr. to secure voting rights for black citizens. During the march, Louis suffered a cracked skull; causing scars he carried the rest of his life. Lewis said, "When you see something that is not right, not just, or not fair, you have a moral obligation to say something or to do something. He also said, "Never be afraid to make some noise and get in good, necessary trouble". Lewis learned early that doing what was right, to be faithful to the truth, required, making "good" trouble. He would need to say things that were unpopular.

The prophet Amos knew this, too. Seeing Israel's sin and injustice, he couldn't keep quiet. Amos denounced how the powerful were oppressing the innocent and taking bribes and depriving the poor of justice in the courts while building stone mansions with lush vineyards, as recorded in Amos 5:11-12. Rather than maintaining his own safety and comfort by staying out of the way, Amos named the evil. The prophet made good necessary trouble. But this trouble aimed at something good~ justice for all. "Let justice roll on like a river!" Amos explained. When we get into good trouble, the kind of righteous, nonviolent trouble justice requires. The goal is always goodness and healing.

Crumb #15: Heavenly Father, if I'm left to myself, I would keep and play it safe. I know that you require something different. Help me discern how to bring you honor and glory.

OUR CHURCH COMMUNITY

Scripture focus: "Let us not give up meeting together, as some are in the habit of doing, but to encourage one another."(Hebrews 10:25)

I grew up the firstborn in the household of Southern Baptist believers. Every Sunday the expectation was clear: I was to be in church with very few possible exceptions. Maybe if I had a severe fever, but the truth is I loved going, and I even went a few times feverish. But the world has changed, and the numbers for a regular church service are not what they used to be. Why? The answers vary. When one pastor was asked, "why do we go to church?" He said, "we go to church for other people, because someone may need you there.

Now, by no means is that the only reason we go to church but his response does resonate with the heartbeat of the writer to the book of Hebrews. He urged the believers to preserve in the faith and to achieve that goal he stressed "not giving up meeting together". Why? Because something vital would be missed in our absence; and it would be difficult to encourage one another. We need that encouragement to "spur one another on toward love and good deeds".

Brothers and sisters keep meeting together because someone may need you there and the corresponding truth is that you may need them as well.

Crumb #16: Heavenly Father as we meet with others to worship and praise your name. Please give us wisdom to also encourage others. Forgive us for being so preoccupied with our personal affairs.

LOOK BEYOND TO FIND THE BEAUTY

Scripture focus: But the Lord said to Samuel, "Do not look at his appearance, or at his physical structure, because I have refused him. For the Lord does not see as man sees for man looks at the outward appearance, but the Lord looks at the heart." (1Samuel16:7).

Cleaning out my bathroom cabinet the other day, I realized something. I have a ton of beauty products. Over the years, I have probably spent more time and money on my appearance than I can remember. From creams to mascara, I seem to have purchased enough to help keep the industry healthy. Part of the reason is I am among those who like to enhance their appearance. Who does not want to look younger and prettier, but this verse is a great reminder of our outward appearance does not matter at all to Jesus. He nurtures the beauty in our hearts.

During Jesus' ministry he came across groups

of people who were concerned with the way they appeared. In Matthew 23, he told the Pharisees "woe to you hypocrite", for you are like white washed stones which, indeed appear beautifully outward, but inside are full of dead man's bones, and all uncleanness." Jesus recognized the deep, spiritual deficiencies ones that only he could fill. And Jesus let them know that he didn't care about their presentation or appearance, but he was concerned about the passion of their hearts.

Crumb #17: Lord, thank you that you only want to look at and continue to nurture the goodness of my heart.

WHO IS THE BUILDER?

Scripture focus: "Unless the Lord builds the house, those who build in labor in vain. Unless the Lord watches over the city, the watchman stays awake in vain." (Psalms 127:1)

In my work over the years, I have seen Jesus guiding my path. He has brought writing and editing products from unexpected sources. He has opened doors in mysterious ways. He has nudged me to change direction sometimes. I've also had times when I planned something in my mind and set out to make it happen. I studied market trends, asked advice of experts, set a course and plowed head with a big dose of stubbornness.

I have designed spreadsheets to chart my progress and searched for an inside track to make my goals happen. None of those are bad techniques, but I've noticed that even though those plans require unending effort, they often fizzle and fail. Looking back, I realized that during some of these periods, Jesus was pointing me to a different path, but I could not hear him over my determination.

When I am building my house or my writing career or my family, or my friendships in my own strength, and not inviting him to do the building, I find myself laboring harder, not smarter. Now, when I catch myself striving, growing resentful at my lack of progress or confused by the way my building keeps crumbling. I stop and ask Jesus if I grabbed the hammer from him. Then I place it back in the Master Carpenter's hands and invite him to direct me in the way that I should go.

Crumb #18 Lord I place my tools in your hands and I thank you for being my master builder and watchman over my life, in Jesus name.

CLOSING

Juliet had known emotional and mental abuse for quite some time now. She was a hard worker and always received accolades. She seemed to get along well with coworkers, friends, and church members. However, in her personal relationship, things were not so well. She always looked to man to validate her, or at least to compliment her, or say something positive. But it never worked– he always reminded her of how terrible she felt about herself.

After months of feeling discouraged, and not good enough, while lying on the floor, and crying out to God for relief, Juliet suddenly felt a calm she never felt before. She heard a voice saying, "I am bringing you out of bondage; out of Egypt". Without knowing why, she got up and went to share what happen with her pastor. I will never forget this experience. It was on a hot Monday evening in July because that previous Sunday,

Juliet had gone into a deep prayer in the spirit at church. She told her pastor that she believed God was giving her instructions to relocate.

From that day to this one, I began to speak to the storms in my life. I told the storms, "You must go now! In the name of Jesus! No weapon formed against me shall prosper! You cannot, and will not defeat me! God told me that I am more than a conqueror through Christ Jesus." That's what I told the storms. Jesus will work it all out. I prayed and pray to my Master, and he answered. The Lord Jesus is my pillar, my high tower, my help, my deliverer, my provider, my advisor, and the Lord of my salvation. I'll continually call on the name of the Lord, who is worthy to be praised. He always hears. Now, I realize that my God, our Father wants to hear from us. He took all of my heart aches and pains. Now, I count my peace of mind as a victory. All the struggles every breath that I take, I've learned to count it all victory.

Abram didn't know where he was going either when God called him to pack up his family and moved to a faraway place. He was seventy-five years old. Abram faced an uncertain future, but he obeyed God and this world will never be the same. We all have a story, and we're right in the middle of it. We can look at it, either with expectant hope, fear, or something in between. But with the perspective of God's truth, we can face the future with joy and boldness.

Prayer strengthens hope as we come to trust the one who knows all. "I know the plans I have for you, declares the Lord, plans to prosper you, and not to harm you, plans to give you a hope and a future." (Jeremiah 29:11) God holds the future. Live in hope!

THE POWER OF A RENEWED MIND

Be transformed by the renewing of your mind. Here comes the emotional roller coaster. Emotions are a normal part of life. As human beings, each of us has a full range of emotions. These emotions, whether positive or negative can be powerful even overwhelming at times. Managing your emotions is a part of maturity. This is where I desperately needed the help of the Holy Spirit. When our emotions are not processed in healthy ways they can get stuck like a clogged drain. Help comes when we surrender our feelings to the one who has the power to blast away our emotional congestion. (Romans 12:2) states do not be conform any longer to the patterns of this world, but be ye transformed by the renewing of your mind. Then you'll be able to prove what is the good and the perfect will of God.

Praying is essential to managing emotions. In fact, it transforms us. (2 Corinthians 10:5) God tells us to "take captive every thought, theory or reasoning and make it obedient to Christ". The biggest crumb knowledge I received here was, to change how we feel we need to adjust the way we think. When we alter the way we view our situations, we can change the way we respond to them with wisdom, rather than impulsive actions. We may regret later. With God's help, we can get through the valleys of our lives.

Crumb of Revelation: Create in me, a heart of compassion, enlarge my vision, so I see and serve the poor, the sick, the people who don't know you, and the people whose concerns you lay upon my heart. Bring me through the dark valleys of confusion and lead me in your direction to an everlasting faithful life. In Jesus name!

IN GOD I TRUST

(Psalms 33:4) "For the word of the Lord holds true and we can trust everything he does."

A person's words are measured by the quality of his or her character. If your friends trust what you say it's because they trust you. If you trust what God says it is because you trust him to be the God he claims to be. If you doubt his word, you doubt the integrity of God himself. We can trust everything he does.

We experience countless feelings every day ranging from exuberant joy to deep grief. God created us with emotions and he knows that they will be part of our walk with Him. Sometimes we feel that God will ignore us because we've messed up. But God is still willing to listen to us. When you feel that your prayers are bouncing off the ceiling, remember that God loves you. He hears and he answers.

David compares God's concern for his people to that of a shepherd. When we allow God to guide us, we experience peace and contentment. Our shepherd knows the "green meadows" and the "peaceful streams" that will the renew us. We will reach these places only by sticking close to him like a sheep would to a shepherd. We should like David, seek God's guidance every day. So when trouble, struggles, or difficult emotions come our way we are already prepared to handle the test. Many of our problems would be avoided or easy to handle if we consistently depend on God's help and direction. Then Jesus said to those who believed him, "If you abide in my word, you are my disciples indeed". (John 8:31)

Crumb of Revelation: When you believe the word of God, the truth, you become a disciple, and this truth you believe makes you free.

BASIC TRAINING/GOD'S TIMING

"He took David from tending the flock and made him the shepherd of Jacob's descendants God's own people, Israel. He cared for them with a true heart, and led them with skillful Hands."(Psalms78:71–72)

God's time frame is a mystery to most of us. Sometimes he seems to move much too slowly. We want everything now, not recognizing that God usually comes at just the right time. God's throne is pictured with a foundation of righteousness and justice. These describe fundamental aspects of the way God deals with people. As God's representatives, we have a responsibility of treating people the way God treats them. Not the way they treated us.

Although David had assumed the throne Israel, he was called a shepherd, not a king. Shepherding, a common profession in biblical times was a highly responsible job. The flocks were completely depended upon shepherds for guidance, provision, and protection. David has spent his early years as a shepherd. Being a shepherd trading for the responsibilities God has in store for him. When he was ready, God took him from caring for sheep to caring for Israel, God's, chosen people.

God is shaping me and you right now for feature responsibilities. Maybe you can't see how doing the same old chores day after day can shape you for a cool purpose. But God can. Faith comes alive at the point where we apply scripture to our lives. The Bible is similar to medicine (now I know) it starts working when it is applied to the areas where it is needed. As you read the Bible, be on alert for lessons, commands, examples, and even "crumbs" from the master's tables that you can apply to every area of your daily life.

Crumb of the Revelation: We become what we are called to be by praying.

Becoming Acquainted with the Author

Matthew 15:26–27 but he answered and said oh, I'm not going to take the children's bread and throw it to the little dogs. And she said yes, Lord, yet even the little dogs eat the crumbs which fall from their masters table. Meet Juliet... Juliet just retired from a successful career in the education system. She is a very well known, highly sought after educator. She is an instructor that has tons of success stories about her students. She's been awarded teacher of the year many times. During her career, she was promoted to education specialist and awarded several supervisory positions. While she is pleasant and competent at the office or at school, Juliet felt lonely and unappreciated. She often isolates herself from having close personal relationships with others.

Prior to receiving the gift of eternal life, one main concept of my personal life was brokenness; which worked hand in hand with loneliness, feeling unloved, and having no sense of direction. I knew about God, but I really didn't take time to get to know him personally. The spirit of rejection and not being good enough haunted me. Because of past hurts and disappointments, every time I faced an upsetting experience, I planned my own course of life. As Max Lucado says, "I was close to the Cross by far from Christ."

Then I receive the gift of eternal life. It was December 7th, my birthday and anniversary. My husband went out to celebrate without his bride. I attended a Bible class in my neighborhood; there I learned to cast my cares on the Lord. The pastor counseled with me and told me that "prayer connects us to the one who has the power to make lasting change in our lives". She explained, "Prayer is a holy conversation, talking and listening to God". She said that "he loves you more much more than you'll ever know". She prayed and then introduced me to Jesus Christ. Then she told me to pray what was in my heart. So I began to confess my sins and asked God for forgiveness. I asked God to please forgive me for all the wrongs I had done, and to give me another chance. I promised in the new chance I would follow his leading and direction. I told him I wanted his wisdom instead of my own.

The gift of eternal life filled me with so much peace. Through prayer and this new knowledge of Jesus Christ I feel loved and secured. I asked God to reshape my life and change me from who I was into the woman He wanted me to be. Now I am learning to trust his ways, not mine. I may not know exactly what will happen next, but I know the one who does know. When you know Jesus in this deeper way, you learn the startling power of God's unconditional love and acceptance, a knowledge that leads us to transformation. It is a wonderful thing to know that forgiveness and transformation are fruits of God's redemption.

Romans 10:9 states "if you can confess with your mouth Jesus is Lord and believe in your heart that God raised him from the dead you will be saved".

If you have never prayed to receive Jesus into your life, why not do so now praying to receive Jesus that your life is the prerequisite to powerful Christian living. Connected to the power of God your prayer life and your entire life will be ignited and energized. That is what gave me the power to write this book, the many, many crumbs of knowledge, and understanding that I have found in Jesus Christ my Savior.

Made in the USA
Columbia, SC
03 November 2024

45249522R00039